# #BlessedMoments

The good, the not so good, and all the
moments in between

Brittany Evans

BookLeaf Publishing

India | USA | UK

Made with ❤ on the BookLeaf Publishing Platform
www.bookleafpub.in
www.bookleafpub.com

# Dedication

To God who has given me many blessed moments and is with me and my family in every moment of every day

# Preface

Every single day we encounter big and small moments that can shape our lives.  My family and I have encountered moments of all sorts: good, really good, bad, and really bad. No matter the moment, God has always been there and will continue to be.  He is truly the reason why some of the most broken moments have such masterpiece endings. He has brought light to the darkest of moments and made the lighter moments even brighter. These poems show how amazing He is and how thankful I am for all of the moments.

# Acknowledgements

Thank you husband, Tootsie, Jackman, Sissy Bear, and K.S. for all the moments in this book and all the many that didn't!

# #EveryMomentCounts

The moments we have in this life can be

lasting
impacting
inspiring
and even disheartening

But it's up to us in how we let these good and not so
good moments define us

We can choose to keep moving even when there is
heartache, anger, and disappointment
We can choose to forgive ourselves and others
We can choose to have more moments with those that
we love and who care about us
We can choose not to check out but to be intentional in
all that we do
We can choose to create positive moments with our
families that are lasting instead of those of the opposite
We can choose to come alongside our children when
they don't understand certain moments of their own life
whether good or not so good
Most importantly we can choose to give all our moments

to God


We all have been blessed with many moments
and whether it's a moment of feeling like you are on top
of the world
or failing miserably
a moment is a moment
and the point is that every time we take a breath we get
to have another moment
And if we get to have another moment
God isn't finished

# #HugTime

Big Brother to Little Sister: Let's do a challenge!
Sister: Okay. Like what?
Brother: Let's see who can go on the floatie the longest.
Mom, can you count?

Mom: Okay, sis goes first.
Brother: But!
Mom: No, ladies first.
Brother: *Eye roll.
Sister: Brother, can you hold it and then I'll tell you let
go.

Brother: Fine.
Sister: Okay! Let go...mom count!
Mom: 1...2
Sister: No mom. Start at 0.
Mom: Okay. 0...1...2...3...

*Meanwhile, brother is splashing and making waves.

Sister: Stop it brother!
Brother: *Looks dumbfounded...What?! I'm not doing
anything.
Mom: 90...91...92...93...94...

Brother: *Sighs...
Mom: 98...99...100!

Sister: Yes! (Splash)
Mom: Way to go Sissybear!
Brother: My turn. Leah, hold it please...okay...let go!
Mom, are you counting?!
Mom: Yes! 10...11...12...
Brother: I can't hear you!

*Meanwhile, sister is splashing and making waves.

Mom: 70...71...72...
Brother: Stop splashing...that's cheating!
Mom: Really? 85...86...87...88
Brother: Woah..steady..steady...
Sister: Yes!

*Meanwhile, the splashing and wave making have
stopped.

Brother: That's not fair. She was distracting me!
Sister: I win!
Mom: It was fair Boo...it was just a game love.

*2 more times later...

Brother: Fine, I'm done.
Mom: Hug Time!
Sister: Yes! Hug Time!
Mom: Let's get him.
Brother: No!

*Mom grabs Brother. Sister latches on. Mom and Sister
rest their heads on Brother and squeeze at the same time.
Brother deflates, smiles, and moments later, they
continue to swim.

These hug time moments are fulfilling and fun, and I'm
hopeful there are many more to come.

# #Adventures

Every family vacation
brings moments
of adventure.


For Example:


lost in the swamp
throw up in the back seat (having to change at the
Pancake House)
nose bleed from the ocean floor
sun burns that make you look like a really ripe tomato
the lack of sunscreen on the back which yielded an
entire bottle of aloe...maybe multiple
run away flip flops into the ocean
oldest child almost taken out by the waves (parents
oblivious)
burying brother in the sand until all you could see was
his face
boogie board riding
wading by dad (which did not end well)
sand in all the places you don't want which becomes
awkward when trying to use the shower at the beach
finding the best shells

taking a walk on the sand with Jackman while losing the
starting point
and...


watching our umbrella fly across the beach
into the bricklebush patch where my husband was the
ultimate champ
he chased after that umbrella and took on those
bricklebushes like no one's business
both hilarious and unfortunate


he may had a few scars when he came out of that patch
along with many strangers observing him with awe
as well as me and the children watching like we were
watching a movie unfold


But!
Curt-1
Umbrella-0.


reconnecting as a family and getting a solid dose of
vitamin sea
are two things that I would never give up because they
create such memories
they are moments that are special, unforgettable, and
brings happiness to the highest degree

not all our adventures have occurred at the beach, and I
know with every fiber of my being, that there is another
one waiting for our family
just within reach

# #Truth

"I Love You."

"No you don't."

"But I do..."

"No you don't or you wouldn't be so mean."

"I'm sorry you feel that way."

"No, you're not sorry."

"I love you."

*child sigh"

"Fine, I love you too."

# #BestTenMinutesEver

morning snuggles are the best

blankie in hand
slobber on face
hair a mess
(and I'm not even talking about me)

"Hi Sissy Bear"

climbs up on lap
rests her head on my chest
cuddles

10 minutes go by
climbs down
plays with dolls

I'll take it

# #Peace

The
best
thing
we
ever
did
for
ourselves
and
our
family
was
saying
yes
to
God.

.

# #Togetherness

Little Sis steps up to the ladder...
    Goggles- Check
    Floaties- Check
    Arms out like Superman- Check
    Counts down
    5
    4
    3
    2
    1
    Woosh!
Big Bro steps up to the ladder...
    No need for any checks other than a goggle
adjustment
    Shouts loudly
    C
    A
    N
    N
    O
    N
    B
    A
    L

L
!
Splash!
Big Sis steps up to the ladder...
Says
"Hand me that float please."
Dad steps up to the ladder...
Backs up a few steps
Runs forwards
Jumps
Grabs Knees
KERPLOSH!
Mom steps up to the ladder...
The temperature of the water determines what
happens next

Moments like these are fleeting
so I'm going to hang on tight to each and every one
while my heart is still beating

# #TheLightWillWin

Some moments can be so dark that it feels as if you can't
breathe and you just want to give up and give in and lie
down

Some moments can be so dark that it feels as if you are
being consumed and the enemy is doing all that He can
to steal any ounce of joy that remains

Some moments can be so dark that if feels as if you are
alone and that even though you are surrounded by
people who love and care it doesn't feel enough

Some moments can be so dark that it feels as if the world
would be a better place without you in it even though
you're being told that's not true

Some moments can be so dark that it feels like you are
not worth it and the bad continually repeats in your
mind

Some moments can be so dark that it feels as if you are
never going to find your way back to the light and that
you might as well just stay in the despair

And...

Watching your child go through this sort of darkness
makes a mother feel so helpless at times

Watching your child go through this sort of darkness
makes a mother fall to her knees and pray harder

Watching your child go through this sort of darkness
makes a mother cling on to the HOPE for the child who
can't seem to grasp it

Watching your child go through this sort of darkness
makes a mother want to swoop in, fix it, make
everything better, hug it out, and then angry because it's
not that easy

But then...

God reminded me that He will heal her...if she lets Him
God reminded me that He will comfort her...if she lets
Him

So...

My prayer is that she will continue to let Him.

# #GodDidIt

The rain had subsided
everyone was seated
Curt wanted to vomit

God brought us together

The birds were chirping
our hands were clammy
two hearts were racing

God brought us together

He let go of my hands
picked up his guitar
sang about our unborn children dancing in my eyes

and once again I knew that God had brought us together

# #I-Do

He woo'd me
loved me
cared about me
and fought for me

which made "I Do" the easiest two words to say

There were tears of joy, excitement, and a little fear
but there was also love, faith, commitment, and an
agreement
that no matter the challenge that would arise we would
stick it out and work it out

which made "I Do" the easiest two words to say

We vowed to love each other everyday
to be each other's advocate everyday
to take care of each other everyday
and to choose each other everyday

Two plus two equals four
and our two "I Do's" led up to the best four words
"You may kiss the bride"

# #HopeForTheFuture

Hope is when you see your child with their hands out
and eyes closed worshipping Jesus.

# #MomFail

The air was thick, with a summer's humid sigh
and a scent of charcoal, where hotdogs and hamburgers
lie
while dad was working the grill, and mom on the inside
working the beans, corn, and American fries

One child enters the kitchen impatiently asking when
din will be done
so mom thought it would be funny reached for a kernel,
only one
directly right out of the pot,
never thinking that it would be hot
or land in her jugular spot

"It's burning, it's burning," she yells with a piercing
scream
shattering the peace that once seemed like a dream
Again..."It's burning, Mama! " the voice sharp and high
a desperate plea looking toward the sky

her hands were up and out begging for help
but all mom could do was stand there and listen to her
yelp
Then mom started a chuckle that was bubbling up from

the soul
but the longer she stood there it began to take a toll

she gained her composure and tried to restrain
but the laughter was rising and was about to pour out
like the rain
And then it unleashed in the most awful way
it was uncontrollable and made mom fall to the floor
laughing where she lay

everything had happened so fast
and after a minute or two mom got herself together at
last
she arose and looked at her daughter in the eyes
with a gentle smirk and a very soft sigh

embraced her daughter with a hug
and then she plucked that corn kernel off with a little tug
But in that moment, etched in my memory's keep
there's a bond of mother-daughter, strong and deep

a simple story, that when told is of pain and glee
of one summer evening and a burning memory
The warmth of corn, the tears, the laughter's sound
this was all a part of a failed mom moment that still to
this day makes me laugh out loud

# #Ezekial36:26

I'll never forget it...

The WORSHIP
The FEELING
The PEOPLE
The RELIEF
The TEARS
The PEACE
The VOICE

JESUS' VOICE

"Brittany, I love you. It's time."

He enveloped me.
He called me by name.
He forgave me.
He loved me.
He restored me.
He was the hope that I needed

"Surrender and give it all to me."

I couldn't do it anymore on my own

I felt His spirit

I was broken
He was the ultimate HEALER

I was angry and ashamed
He was the ultimate FORGIVER

I was sad
He was the COMFORTER

I didn't trust
He sought me ought

I was difficult
The answer was simple

All He wanted was me
I listened


This moment TRANSFORMED me.

# #NotPromisedAnotherDay

4:30 PM I was holding Gram's hand.
4:35 PM Grams wakes up.

Grams: "Hey Tootsie."
Me: "Hi Grams."
Grams: "How are you today?"
Me: "I'm good Grams."
Grams: "How are the babies?"
Me: "They're good Grams."
Grams: "I love you tootsie."
Me: "I love you too Grams."

4:50 PM Grams fell asleep.

The next morning...

7:15 AM I received a phone call.

Me: "Hello"
Mom: "Honey, I'm so sorry. Grandma passed away last night."

4:35 PM almost didn't happen because I was tired from work.

4:35 PM was the last moment Grams called me "Tootsie."

4:35 PM was the last moment that I was able to see my favorite person.

4:35 PM was the last moment that I was able to talk to my favorite person.

4:35 PM was the last moment that I was able to touch my favorite person.

4:35 PM was the last moment that I heard my Grams say she loved me.

4:35 PM will always be a moment that I cherish forever.

# #Teamwork

The year 2019 brings me back to the beautiful morn
 that our third baby Leah was born


And even though this moment was one that we are so
thankful to have
the moments leading up to this miraculous day
were not so beautiful because the contents of my
stomach would never stay


9 months of getting sick morning, noon, and night
coming home leaning on Curt to make everything else
right
while I was in the bathroom and out of sight


Everyday I would:
Wake up
Get sick
Go to work (stop at Thornton's to get sick on the way)
Teach (occasionally stopping to go to the bathroom to
get sick)
Go home (trying to not pull over)
Love the children and husband up
Get sick
Rest

Get sick
Try to eat what the husband cooked
Get sick
Go to bed
Wake up and repeat for the next 8 months

7 days a week for all of those months felt like I was on replay
but my husband and children went out of their way
to help me without complaining each and every day

I thought the last 6 months might get better
and at this point I was definitely not a go-getter
and the response to "Why is mom sleeping again?" my husband would reply "Just let her".

5 times an hour I would pray at least
for all of the sickness to subside and cease

4 little words that entered my mind after visiting the lou
were "She is worth it" which is 100% the truth

3 days overdue
with many conversations with God questioning whether
or not He already knew

2 contractions came and went, and at that moment,

I told my husband exasperatedly that I hope this was it

1 more night and morning of hard pain and getting sick
that eventually led to one of the most precious God
given gifts

Without my husband, my Lilly, Jackman, and my
students who would bring me Cheerios
you are the real MVPs of those 9 months
and those memories I will never let go

# #TurningPoint

The turning point
of
our marriage
took place
in our
living room
where
the decision
had to be made...


Are we going to get a divorce?
or
Are we going to stay married?


Are we going to give up and give in?
or
Are we going to keep going?


Are we going to live in the past?
or
Are we going to look to the future?

Are we going to choose ourselves?

or

Are we going to choose each other?


We chose US.

# #ALittleChat

Ten at night and a child enters the living room
somber, lost, and needing attention
so I push pause on the remote control
and get ready to give some love and affection

"Buddy, what's wrong" I say
as his tears hit the floor
"Talk to me love"
although my heart didn't know what was in store

"I just feel sad and I feel as if no one wants me around"
Knees up, head down, crying those crocodile tears
"I love you so much"
Holding hands to draw him near while trying to calm his
fears

"I want you around kid"
"You're my mom, that doesn't count"
"Are you kidding me? I'm the one that counts the most
and we all love you and so does God, that's something
you should never doubt"

*Hug

When the hug was over and we talked about all the
feelings
he started to feel better
I reminded him that he in fact is never alone
and our family is doing this life together

Thank you God for moments that are tender
Thank you God for moments that require a really long
hug
Thank you God for moments that remind us how lucky
we are to have one another
and Thank you God for moments that give the heart a
tug

# #AMotherKnows

It started out just like any other day
the annoying and persistent alarm going on and on
the birds chirping outside
the sun shining through the windows making it seem
warm

Everyone was getting ready for work and school
the beautiful brown haired and brown eyed girl watching
Lady in the Tramp
dad getting his coffee
and I had changed my clothes for the tenth time

And out of nowhere, there was a feeling that showed up
that I couldn't shake
it was a weird feeling that scared me but yet at the same
time I didn't recognize it
this feeling was sad and uncomfortable
I remember thinking that I should say something to Curt
but I pushed it aside and we all left for the day

Or so I thought I pushed it aside...

All the way to work all I could do was feel this feeling
and no matter how hard I tried to ignore it and move on

this feeling kept rearing its ugly head
and finally I knew

Because a mother knows...

An expectant mother of her second child knows...

I knew something was very wrong
I knew that I needed to go check
I knew that what I saw in the bathroom wasn't right
I knew, but I didn't want to know...

When I got home and it was getting worse
I knew I needed to go into the hospital
but I didn't want to go alone
so I waited

I was clinging on to the HOPE that I was wrong
that the baby was okay
and that what I was experiencing could be normal
I was HOPING

But I knew...

I went into the bathroom one last time before it was time
to leave
and all of a sudden there was a pain that overtook me

I remember crouching over and crying
yes it was excruciating but it wasn't just the physical
pain that was overtaking me

It was the pain that only a mother would know seeing
the unborn child not where they're supposed to be

I knew that even though I had not been with this child
for more than 12 weeks I loved him very much
I knew that this would be the last time I saw my baby
until I went to Heaven too

I didn't know the why but I knew that God did and that
He had me
I knew that He loved me
and even though the sadness was unbearable and
consumable
I could still feel God's presence trying to comfort me

He knew I was going to need reminders of His love for
me
to keep my faith growing strong
to be able to cope
and to be able to keep moving when all I wanted to do
was lay in bed and put the covers over my head

I found myself at church the next Sunday even though I

didn't want to go

my husband was worshipping so I thought maybe it
would be good for me

and Lilly could see Grandma Julie and be around people
who seemed more alive than me

and then worship started and Curt started to sing to
God...

"Higher than the mountains that I face

Stronger than the power of the grave

Constant through the trial and the change

One thing remains, yes, one thing remains

Your love never fails

It never gives up

It never runs out on me

Your love never fails

It never gives up

It never runs out on me

Your love never fails

It never gives up

It never runs out on me

Because on and on, and on, and on it goes

Before it overwhelms and satisfies my soul

And I never, ever, have to be afraid

One thing remains, yes, one thing remains

your love" -Jesus Culture

I dropped to my seat and just started to cry out in prayer
my heart was sick but in that moment I felt the Holy
Spirit consume me
telling me He is with me and that
His love won't fail and it will get me through

My husband was crying on stage, I was crying in my seat
and we were mourning together
and God was comforting us

Later that evening we went to our marriage group
even though I told Curt, again, I didn't want to go
once again I went anyways
I had so many emotions and was exhausted and I didn't
want to people

I remember everyone being so kind and loving
and eventually it got to be too much
I got up to go into the kitchen just so I could breathe
because even though I could actually breathe I felt as if I
was being suffocated
I was just standing there trying to breathe when Wendy
walked in

She came over to me
hugged me
put her hands on my belly

and prayed for me

I've never been prayed for like that in my life until this
point
and this prayer of healing and thankfulness was the most
powerful prayer
I had ever experienced
and then to follow up she gave me the kind of hug that
makes you want to melt

It was okay to cry
It was okay to be sad
It was okay to be mourn
It was okay because I knew God had me

This moment in time was an ugly one for me
but it was also beautiful because looking back I can see
God's love and faithfulness and how He used the people
around me

Three months had gone by and I knew...

A mother always knows...

Our family of three would soon no longer be

# #NoWordsNeeded

Few words are needed
because your best friend just knows
by looking at you

# #NerfsUp

Nerf War, the battle of foam,
Where the children's laughter echoes, and many tactics roam.
With blasters in hand, day or night,
We are ready to charge into the fray with might.
Oh, the thrill of the dart, the sting of the hit,
A dance of dodging, never quite fit.
From the shadows, or bathroom, we creep, with strategy keen,
To the living room, our battlefield scene.

They are the mighty Elite, compact and small,
But each has a weapon, to make him fall.
They stealthily paused until mom made the first move,
The kids knew what to do as soon as soon as the first bullet flew.
Mom targeted dad as he sat in his chair,
And he didn't know what was coming, specifically the bullet, that was about to fly through the air.
As he looked up, and made eye contact with mom; he thought there was nothing to dread,
But then the bullet hit, WHAM, right in the middle of his forehead.

We unleashed the fury with triggers so fast,
And it's so awesome that we wanted the moment to last.
10 rounds later mom and dad started to get tired,
So they had to talk the kids into a cease fire.
We told the kids that if you start to miss it and are
feeling glum,
Try not to worry because there are many more nerf
moments in this life to come.
Children always have your NERF blasters ready, and
wait for the battle to commence,
But in the meantime don't forget to think about what
team to be on and about mom's amazing defense.

# #FutureMoments

In moments to come, I choose...

to go into this new year
trusting God and knowing that He will always be near

to believe that no matter what comes our way
our family will be able to stand our ground, together,
without going astray

to embrace all that God has in store
whether big or small and all the other things that will try
to get thrown our way that we must endure.

to remember when I feel like I don't have what it takes
and the light is becoming dim
that I need to look to Jesus because He will remind me
that I can do it through Him

to be bold and pray with others
and to show that Jesus' love is like no other

to be intentional with helping my children grow in their
relationships with Jesus, too
by loving my family more fervently and passionately

while teaching them about God's truths

to go through these future moments knowing that God is
with us
and that no matter where we go the goal should be to
shine the light of Jesus.